For Zoë, Felix, Cash, and Wren

www.enchantedlion.com

First published in 2025 by Enchanted Lion Books,
248 Creamer Street, Studio 4, Brooklyn, NY 11231

ISBN: 978-1-59270-411-8

A CIP record is on file with the Library of Congress

Printed in China by R.R. Donnelley Asia Print Solutions

First Edition

FSC www.fsc.org MIX Paper | Supporting responsible forestry FSC® C144853

THE FORGOTTEN TEACHERS

How Nature Wrote the Story of Life

BRIAN ISETT

CLAUDIA BIÇEN

unruly
an Enchanted Lion Book
NEW YORK

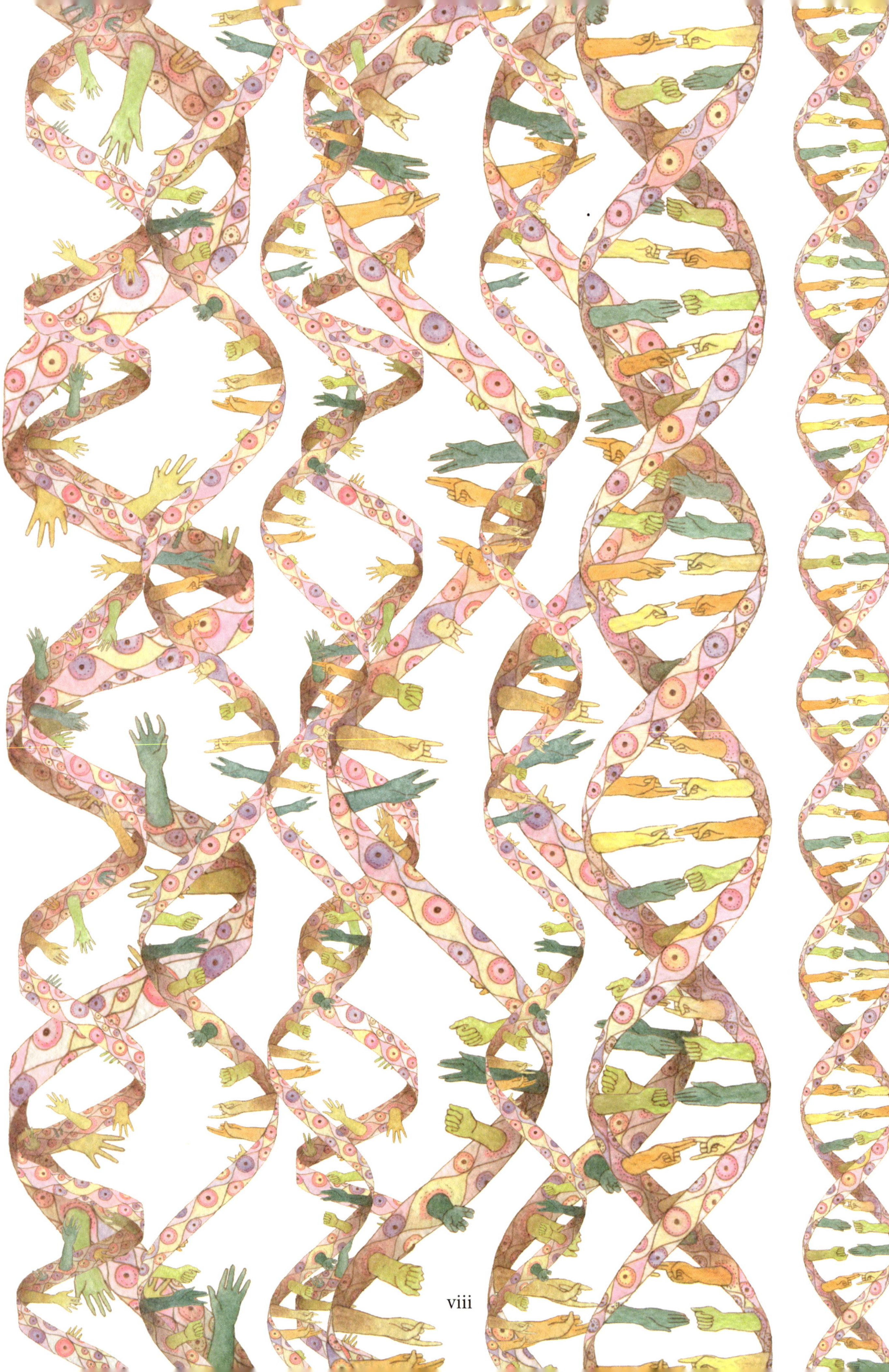

INTRODUCTION

What is DNA? When the term comes up, we might think of something central to who we are, or picture a long, twisting molecule packed with information. And both of these thoughts would be correct. But DNA also contains something incredible that we are just beginning to understand: our DNA contains a story. In part, that's because our DNA can be thought of as an ancient form of text. Let's take a look at some of it right now:

AGCCGTTACCTGCAGCTGATGAGCTCCAAAAGAGCGAAACCTATT
GGTCCTGCAGTACTGGCT

The A's, G's, C's, and T's written above correspond to adenine, guanine, cytosine, and thymine—the chemical letters, or "nucleotides," that spell out each long strand of our DNA. "Genes" are what we call the distinct strings of these same four chemical letters. The text above represents a gene for the hammerhead ribozyme, and it is one of the most ancient pieces of genetic text ever to be discovered.

Some genes are instructions for making tiny building blocks in the body called "proteins." Other genes, like the hammerhead ribozyme, make an active molecule from the genetic text itself. The ribozyme performs its action by folding into a loop that can cut other strings of genetic text into two separate strands. Think of it as an ancient form of the space bar, which, by separating characters, turns a long string of nucleotide letters into two fragments.

This gene is in our bodies, and it is also found in nearly every organism alive on Earth. Because it is so widespread, scientists think it evolved before cells, and even before DNA itself (the gene was originally written in the form of an even older text called "RNA"). That would make this piece of genetic text approximately four billion years old.

Now, the hammerhead ribozyme is very old, and that means it hasn't changed much over time. This is because the gene, in being very small and important, can't have many letters change if it's to keep working correctly. By contrast, other genes change relatively quickly, and in the process, they may turn into something altogether new. This happens through small changes in the spelling of a gene, which occur mostly by chance across generations. These misspellings are called "mutations." Some mutations are harmful and cause disease; for example, many forms of cancer are caused by misspelled genes. Other mutations do nothing at all. But a few mutations prove very helpful, sometimes to such a degree that an organism and the organism's offspring are more likely to thrive with the new mutation than without it. As a result, a helpful mutation encourages organisms toward keeping that new spelling. As mutations accumulate across generations, organisms begin to change as a whole, contributing to a process called "evolution."

By understanding what genes do and how they evolved, we begin to get a detailed picture that tells us about the history of life on Earth. We can better understand our ancestors and the evolutionary challenges those ancestors faced, and even discover our deepest connections to Earth and the more-than-human world. Slowly, certain themes start to emerge. Genes like the hammerhead ribozyme provide a hint about what it was like when life began billions of years ago in the ocean, and there are many other genes that point to that time as well. Collectively, they tell a story about one hidden figure impacting all of biology: Ocean. Ocean is an immense natural force that has repeatedly shaped our biology and experiences over time. But the entirety of life wasn't shaped by the teachings of Ocean alone.

Let's meet the rest of our forgotten teachers.

By poring over biological research, we identified dozens of potential teachers: Sun, Predators, Plants, Shadows, Air, Death, and many more. In the process, we noticed that some teachers tend to attract, or "pull" life toward a teaching, while others repel, or "push" life away. For example, the Sun pulls organisms toward its teachings by providing energy, warmth, and light for vision. By contrast, the threatening lessons of Predators and Death push organisms away from telling a certain story. For example, Predators push animals away from displaying bright colors that make them easy to find, often resulting in a subtle camouflage to better blend into the environment. Pushing and pulling forces are equally important to the evolution of life, but in this book, we chose to focus on the forces that pull. From the teachers that have these pulling effects on creatures, we chose six: Ocean, Air, Theia (an ancient planet), Sun, Plants, and Symbionts (the organisms involved in symbiosis). Each of these forgotten teachers left indelible lessons in our DNA and taught each species a particular piece of the story that unites all of life. When examined as a whole, this story describes the unique and ancient tale of what it is like to live and thrive on Earth, of what it is like...

...to emerge from Ocean's aquatic depths, carrying lessons on writing genetic text and making cells...

...to breathe Air and connect to the fundamental cycle of growth, sustenance, and decay...

...to live on a planet that, after its collision with Theia, forever hums with clear temporal rhythms of days, months, and seasons...

...to live under Sun's bright light and evolve the ability to see...

...to have our senses expanded by the colors, smells, and tastes of Plants...

...to become so interdependent with Symbionts that what is "us" and what is "them" becomes forever blurred into a unified whole.

This grand, ancient story has shaped all of us, along with the rest of the natural world, and together we make up the living, breathing edge of this tale. Each creature—human, insect, frog, coral, songbird, tree—carries its own unique, irreplaceable perspective on the deep history of Earth. Yet today, many of these creatures are going extinct at an accelerating rate, largely due to human activity and the refusal to accept a more holistic view of life. Despite this being our only home, and despite the story of life we share, connecting us all, we seem to have forgotten how to tell stories filled with wonder, awe, and a sense of mystery.

It's time for us to remember.

MEMENTO OBLITA

CHAPTERS

OCEAN

Once upon a time, Ocean taught life how to begin. The lesson began somewhere warm, like the shallow waters of a calm bay, or the billowing broth of a hydrothermal vent. In these places, warm water provided enough energy to link up chemicals that normally stayed apart. Rings of carbon, called "nucleotides," clumped together just the way letters do to make words. And while most of the clumps formed nonsensical tangles, some formed babbling threads of an early genetic text called "RNA." With Ocean's encouragement, a chain reaction began: instead of dissolving back into the sea, chemicals began to fold into delicate structures that enabled even more chemical reactions to take place. These early molecules, many now called "ribozymes," are thought to have sustained the first whispers of life. Our story had begun.

These chemical structures were, however, still quite fragile. Slight changes in the water—perhaps growing too hot from energy, too sour from acids, or too bitter from bases—could quickly break the molecules apart, erasing their texts. What our earliest chemical ancestors needed was a safe place to write freely. Something like a tiny ocean within Ocean, even just a drop. Now, it just so happens that oily droplets of chemicals called "phospholipids" can easily collect into hollow spheres when they encounter water, and so it was into that protected space that our earliest chemical ancestors moved their writing. Once they did, they became unstoppable. Today, we call these spaces "cells," and our bodies are made of billions of them.

Inside these first cells, our earliest ancestors drafted and composed. New genes began to emerge: genes about cell division and genes about sensing the outside world from the inside of an oily bubble. Cells divided and cells joined together. Changes began to accumulate at a rapid pace: single-celled organisms multiplied into multicellular animals, such as sponges, anemones, and worms. These forms led to boneless creatures with spinal cords; to fish with skeletons, but no jaws; to fish with jaws and fins; then to fish with lungs and fins, strong enough to hop through puddles on land—lungfish, which still exist today; and eventually to something not quite a fish anymore—an amphibian. Amphibians turned fins into legs, and the exploration of land had begun.

Even as our ancient amphibian ancestors left Ocean to explore dry land, they still carried a blueprint of Ocean as they went, as evidenced by the fact that all baby vertebrates have an aquatic start. Fish and amphibians still lay their eggs in water, of course, but even birds, reptiles, and mammals recreate an aquatic environment by using a sac of amniotic fluid. Like ocean water, the salty amniotic fluid cushions a fetus from injury and provides an osmotic gradient—a state that allows water, nutrients, and waste to more easily be exchanged between the embryo and its surrounding environment. As such, amniotic tissue tells a clear story about how life carried the lessons of Ocean onto dry land, maintaining a wet environment for embryos everywhere our ancestors went.

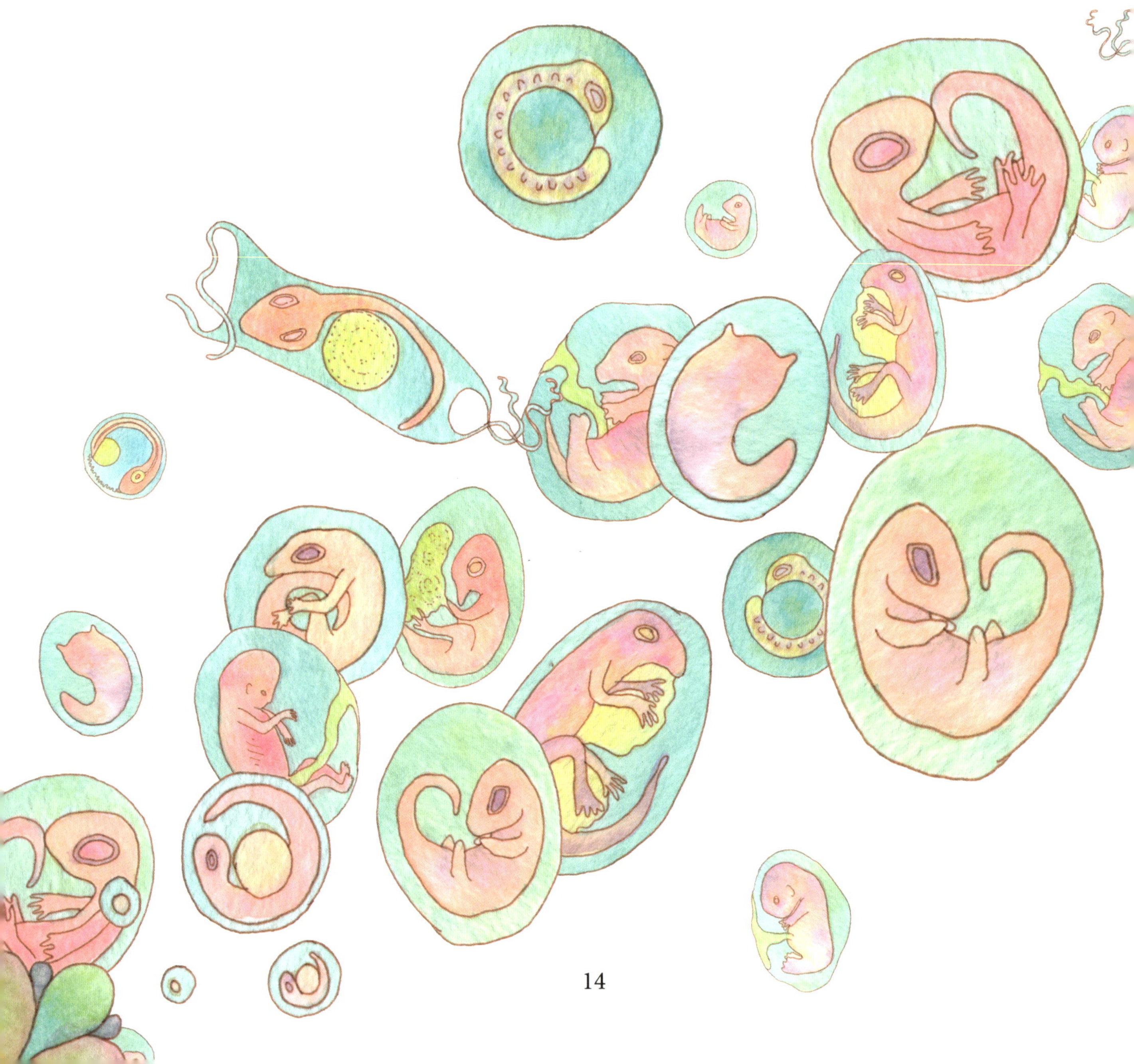

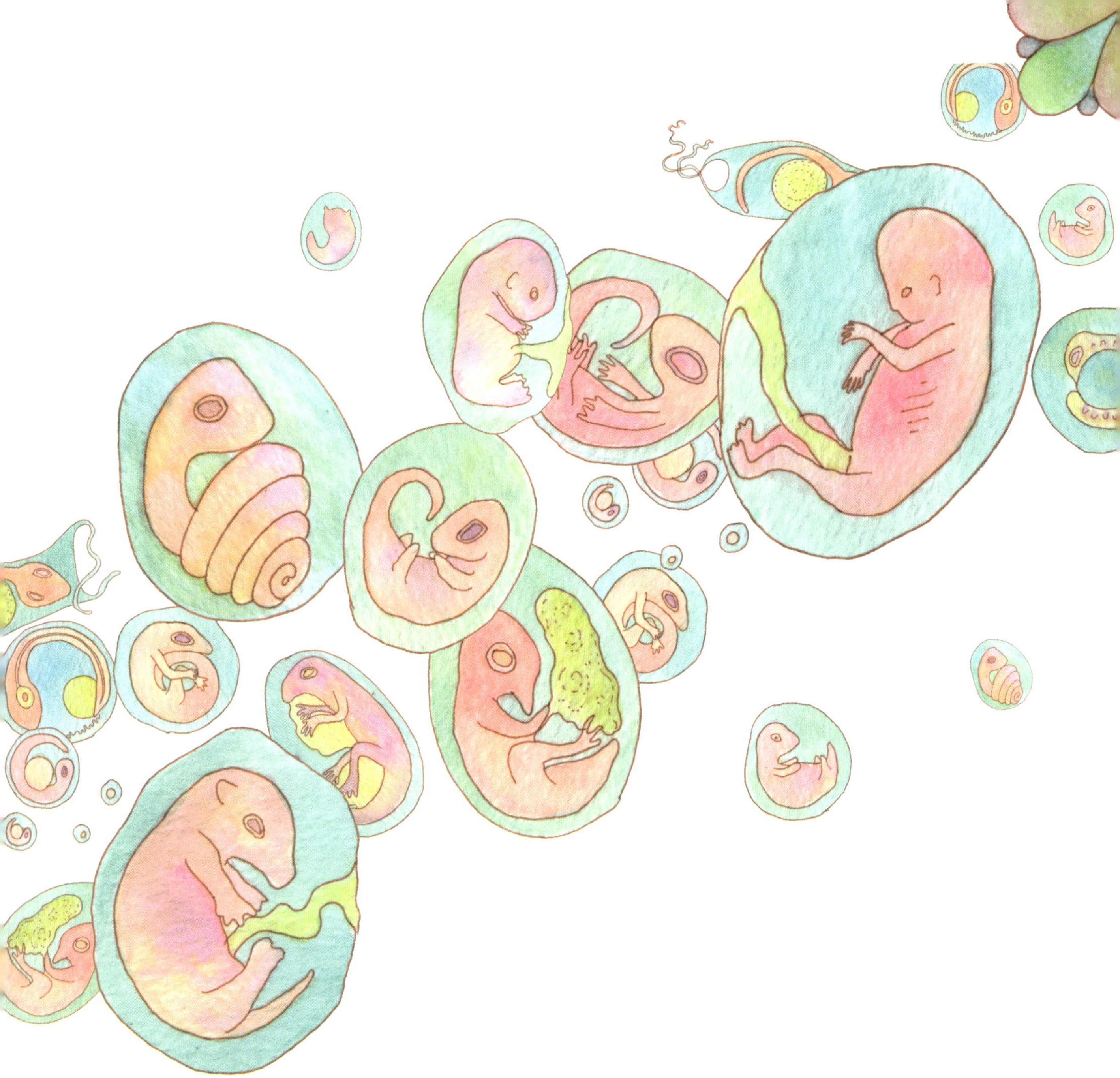

As human embryos floating in our mothers' wombs, our necks still form the place where gills once developed: small bumps called "pharyngeal arches," which in fish become the gills and jaw. In mammals, they now become the lower jaw and a part of the neck and the middle ear. The middle ear allows us to amplify and sense sound in the air, and it was only recently discovered that this important area evolved from ancient gills, just like our jaw and even our voice box. The use of amniotic fluid and the presence of pharyngeal arches are just two of Ocean's ancient lessons that our bodies still retell today.

When our mothers made us, they too cupped a pocket of brine from genetic memory and created an Ocean in their wombs. In doing so, each mother's body remembers and repeats the ancient story passed down from her mother and her mother's mother, all the way back to Ocean, the first mother of us all, inscribing in us the earliest story of life.

Now, while Ocean is mother of us all and has taught us many lessons, it still might be said that Ocean had only one immediate descendant. Among the untold billions of cells swarming in the early Ocean, there was only one single cell, with only one story of Ocean, that branched into all the creatures alive today. That cell is known as "LUCA," the Last Universal Common Ancestor. We are all descendants of LUCA, with no breaks or gaps of any kind. This lineage connects us directly to the beginning of life, and four billion years later, these shared ancient lessons still travel with us, wherever we go. As we hike through Earth's driest deserts or climb her coldest mountain peaks, we bring a hint of Ocean to places Ocean could never reach alone.

AIR

By leaving Ocean for land, our ancestors encountered a new teacher rushing overhead: Air. Because it is invisible, it's easy to forget that Air is like a second ocean; clouds float in it like icebergs and birds swim through it like fish. Air's weather gives us fresh water, and through the carbon dioxide it contains, Air also provides the raw material for our physical bodies. Each breath of Air we take connects us to an ancient cycle of growth, sustenance, and decay, a series of teachings scientists call "the fast carbon cycle."

The cycle begins with growth. Self-sufficient organisms like Plants grow at the base of the global food chain, using water, sunlight, soil, and Air. While it might seem as though a plant is formed from water and soil, a plant's shape actually comes from Air. The magic of turning Air into forms is called "photosynthesis." "Photo-" refers to the use of sunlight to power the process, and "-synthesis" refers to building new chemical shapes that allow Plants to grow, a process that also releases oxygen. And as they grow, Plants spin the carbon dioxide in Air into sugars, which can be used to make fruits, leaves, and even DNA. For many creatures, these offshoots became sources of nutrition.

Taking all of these properties together, we might say photosynthesis opens a portal between formlessness and form. Carbon dioxide, which was once invisible, blowing aimlessly in the wind, passes through the portal of photosynthesis and gives shape to a plant. On the physical side of the portal, we can touch the waxy leaves made from Air and smell Air's new plant fragrance. And because what we eat is ultimately something built from the sugars and starches of Plants, our own form results from traveling through this portal. We, too, are made from Air.

But what is Air? Today, Air is mostly made of nitrogen and oxygen, with small amounts of carbon dioxide and other gases mixed in. However, the mixture of gases that makes up Air is always changing. Before life emerged, there was so little oxygen in Air that we couldn't have even lit a match. That began to change two billion years ago, when the single-celled creatures in Ocean had performed enough photosynthesis to fill Air across the whole planet with oxygen. Rocks with iron inside began to rust for the first time, a process that only occurs when iron is exposed to moisture and oxygen. Indeed, the rust was so widespread that a red layer formed in the geological record in what is now called the "Great Oxygenation Event." This ancient rust remains the source of much of our iron ore today.

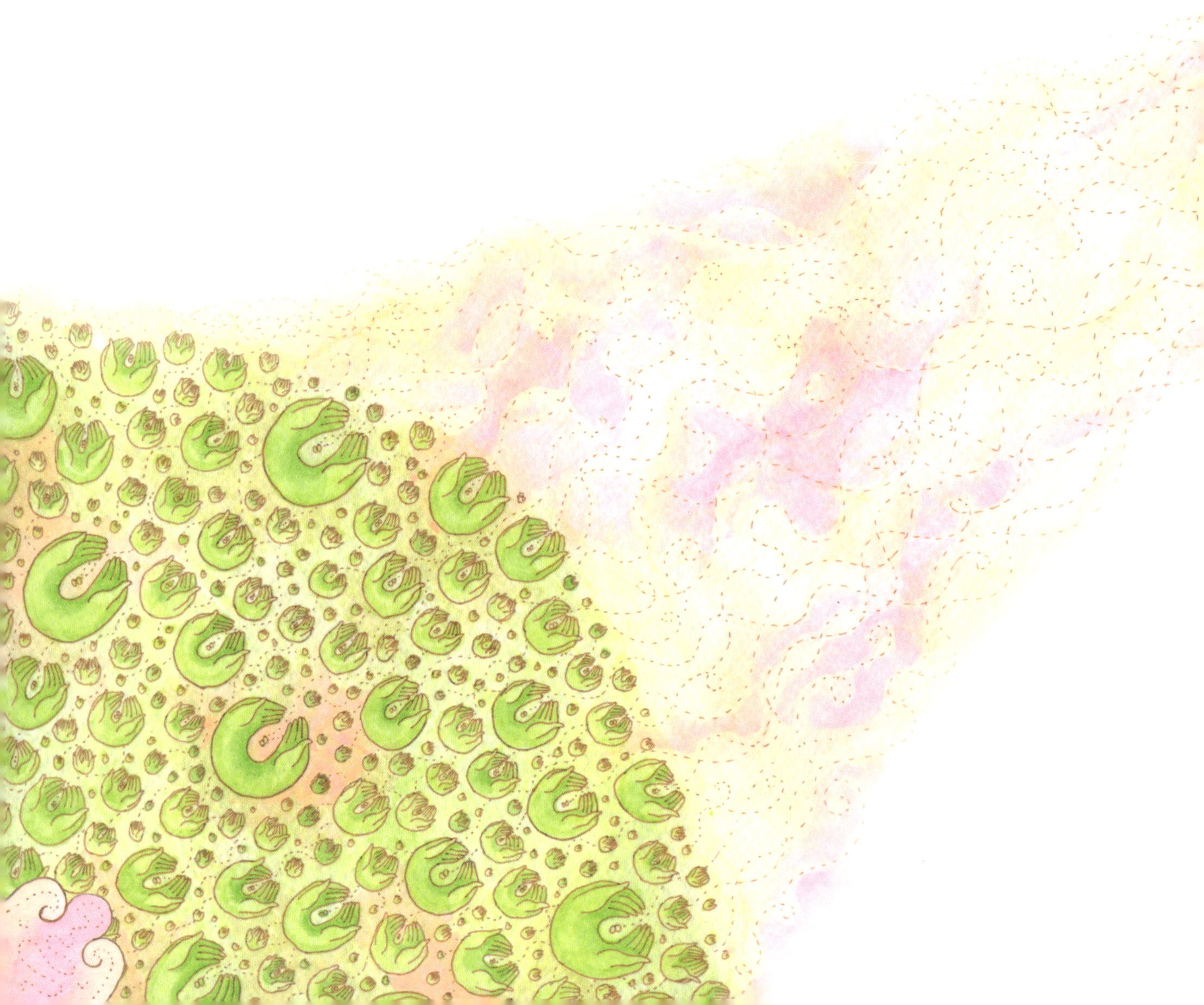

All the same, we still couldn't have lit a match back then. Oxygen from photosynthesis had to accumulate for another two billion years before Earth's first wildfires began, around 420 million years ago. This is the first moment when plant charcoal, the black carbon residue left behind after a fire, can be found in the fossil record. It took trillions and trillions of small photosynthetic sighs for Plants and plankton to make Air that we can breathe, with enough oxygen to burn wood.

Our bodies are also sustained by something like a fire burning inside them. Our fire is called "metabolism," a term capturing the many ways our bodies create and consume energy. Like a fire, our metabolism is sustained by oxygen from Air. In both cases, oxygen helps pull apart the elements of carbon-rich fuel: in a fire, this carbon-rich fuel is wood, but in our metabolism, the fuel is the food we eat. Amazingly, the by-products of fire and metabolism are nearly identical: both release carbon dioxide, water, and energy in the form of heat and light. Carbon dioxide and water vapor are in each breath we exhale, and the heat we produce keeps our bodies warm. The light we emit falls within the infrared spectrum, giving us each a soft glow. While this glow is invisible to us, it is obvious to creatures like bullfrogs, salmon, pit vipers, and mosquitoes, who can all see or detect the infrared light of our metabolic fire.

Unlike a wood fire, however, our bodies channel some of this energy away from heat and light and into the chemical bonds of a miraculous chemical called "adenosine triphosphate" (ATP). ATP powers everything our bodies do, from healing a burn to moving our muscles as we take a deep breath. And we take a breath every four seconds, which

amounts to 20,000 breaths a day. Each breath connects us to the wider breathing world and energizes our cells. Every four seconds, Air reminds us that we are not separate from the world, but made from it and sustained by it. Through our breath, we participate in Air's currents, expanding our presence beyond our bodies, perhaps through a hum or a joyous shout.

After our very first breath of Air as an infant, we cry. This initial shock of breath in the lungs is followed by a soothing repetition that can amount to 600 million breaths over a lifetime. But inevitably, the hum of life falls silent for each of us when we die. The final lesson we are taught is that each of our bodies will return to Air when we are gone. Following death, fungi and microbes break down our physical forms and return them back to Air as carbon dioxide.

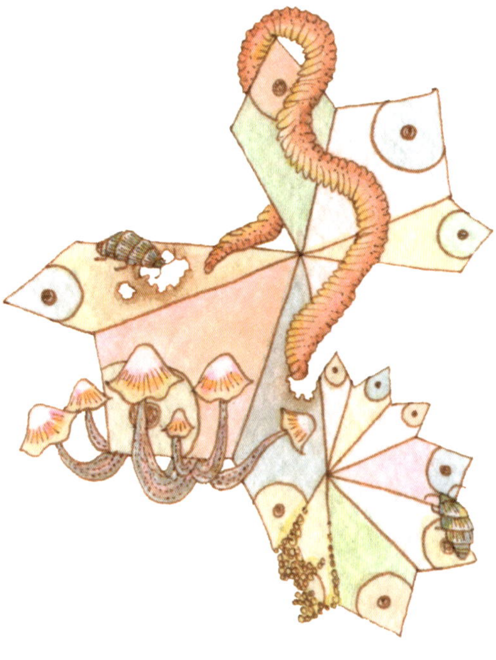

Now, the cycle is complete: growth, sustenance, and decay. Air teaches life something about each process. We grow from a food chain that relies on Air; we are sustained by Air's oxygen; and we each return to Air when our body eventually decays. But a cycle is never truly over. A cycle carries us beyond every ending: after decay, Plants breathe our carbon back into their leaves, and the cycle begins once again.

THEIA

Feeling every rhythm on Earth, life slowly learned to dance. The Sun drops below the horizon as day cools to night; Ocean's waves touch dry sand at high tide; and Air fills with golden leaves as summer turns to autumn, heralding winter. Our ancient ancestors learned to sense time from these earthly cycles of temperature and light: when to sleep, when to eat, when to set out on a journey. But none of these cycles would have been the same without one of the most forgotten teachers of all: Theia. Theia, named after the Titan from Greek mythology who gave birth to the Sun, Moon, and Dawn, was an ancient planet about the size of Mars that started Earth's orchestra of temporal rhythms with something of a bang.

Four-and-a-half billion years ago, back when Earth was still hot and new, Theia slipped into Earth's orbital path. The two planets collided, creating an impact so intense that it knocked Earth onto a tilt and sent it spinning on its axis toward the Sun. As the molten rock of these fused planets cooled, the leftover pieces formed the Moon, and all of Earth's most dependable rhythms began. Earth's spin brought day and night, Earth's tilt brought the seasons, and the Moon brought light to the night sky and pulled the tides, marking months. Today, two huge chunks of Theia rest deep in Earth's mantle, under the Pacific Ocean and the continent of Africa. Both of these chunks are characterized by a distinct mineral signature.

As our ancestors experienced Earth's rhythms drumming across millions of years, many rhythms also entered into the genetic stories of our DNA. In the case of Earth's spin, these stories are called "circadian rhythms," and they describe patterns of behavior and biological activity that follow the 24-hour cycle of day and night. Like dancers, we move to this rhythm, inspired by its timing but not locked to it. Nearly all organisms contain a circadian rhythm, from bacteria and Plants to fungi and animals.

Under the protective darkness of night, many animals sleep. And while we sleep, we may begin to dream. Neuroscience research suggests that dreams may be our brains determining which memories to forget and which to keep. This process allows us to simplify what we've experienced during the day and frees up the brain to make new associations. It must be very important to dream, because nearly every mammal (and even some birds and invertebrates, like jumping spiders) experiences REM, or "rapid-eye-movement," sleep. This is the period of sleep when our most intense dreams occur. One of the animals that gets the most REM sleep, the duckbill platypus, even looks dreamlike! This unusual mammal experiences 8.5 hours of REM while sleeping 14 hours a day. We don't know if they spend that time dreaming, but if they do, they spend almost as much time in the dreamworld as they do awake.

Riding under the flicker of night and day, one of Theia's longer rhythms begins to emerge. The Moon, made of leftover pieces of Theia and Earth, completes one lunar cycle every 29.5 days. This is called the "lunar month," and it is the reason we still have months in our calendar today. During the lunar month, the Moon emerges from Earth's shadow as a thin crescent, and then fills to a full Moon in about two weeks' time. Over the subsequent two weeks, it gradually empties of light, returning to Earth's shadow to begin again as a new Moon. At the same time, the Moon also pulls Ocean through a complete cycle of high and low tides.

Life listened to these rhythms closely. So much so that many creatures evolved circalunar rhythms (rhythms that respond to moonlight) and circatidal rhythms (rhythms that respond to tides). Coastal mangrove crickets, for example, have a strong circatidal clock that tightly locks to the rhythm of high and low tide, but not day and night. They take cues from how flooded the ground is to set their pace.

Many fish also use lunar rhythms to recognize tidal patterns. For example, the grunion of southern California can recognize the spring and summer nights with the highest tides, which occur on nights with a new or full Moon. When these nights arrive, grunions catch a large set of waves and beach themselves on the sandy shore to lay their eggs. With the next wave, they are gone, washed back into the ocean. Grunions have felt these tidal rhythms for millions of years, holding within their DNA a story of what it's like when the California coasts they call home align just right with the Sun and the Moon.

After several lunar months, Earth begins to change seasons. The tilt Theia imparted to Earth is slight, only 23.5 degrees, but it is enough to heat the Earth in summer and cool it in winter, depending on which hemisphere leans toward the Sun during Earth's annual orbit. Plants and animals sense the changing seasons, taking cues from the environment: the amount of daylight, the temperature, the amount of rain. As days lengthen in spring, Plants push toward leaf and bloom, while birds erupt into song at dawn. In autumn, trees prepare for winter by draining their leaves of photosynthetic pigments, turning them brilliant shades of red and yellow before letting them go. Thanks to the Earth's tilt, staying in one place paradoxically guarantees change. Even near the equator, where the tilt has the least influence, there are seasons of rain, like the monsoons. To counterbalance these seasonal changes, many animals evolved to migrate. Fish swim, birds fly, and in the past, humans roamed, often following herds of animals like bison or caribou.

Imagine living off the land 5,000 years ago. After months of foraging, hunting, and harvesting, the whole community stops to rest, like monarch butterflies overwintering in colonies on the branches of oyamel firs. This year, there has been plenty of food and everyone is prepared for winter. Friends and family gather to give thanks, celebrating this good fortune in a tradition that extends back in various forms to a time before written history. This tradition continues today in holidays like Thanksgiving in the United States and the New Yam (Iri-ji) Festival in West Africa, as well as dozens of other celebrations around the globe. Many animals also change their social behaviors with the seasons, forming colonies around food availability and optimal conditions for raising their young. While these colonies are not technically celebrations in human terms, it is nearly impossible to watch a beach full of elephant seals who have gathered to raise pups in winter without noticing a festive mood. In that spirit, Theia's final lesson is to come together as the seasons change. Through gathering, we find the warmth, community, and good cheer that sustain us in an ever-changing world.

SUN

Each morning, Sun rises from the horizon, warming the Earth and waking a tide of activity in the creatures below. Sun provides the light necessary for photosynthesis and illuminates the rhythms of Theia. But there is an even bigger lesson from Sun that we often forget: Sun taught us to see the world around us. Nearly all organisms on Earth sense or react to light, from bacteria and algae to Plants and animals. In fact, 96 percent of animal species have eyes, the highly specialized sensory organs for processing light into vision. Our eyes reveal a world filled with colors, edges, and shadows that coalesce into vivid visual imagery, like the distinct appearance of an edible plant or the faint hint of an approaching predator. Images capture the beauty of our world, as though Sun has been proclaiming one ancient, shining lesson: this is a place worthy of being seen.

How is it that Sun has taught so many creatures to see? It turns out that the evolutionary paths to vision had a few common steps that many creatures have taken: detect light, make a spot, pinch it into a cup, and add a lens.

To detect sunlight, Sun taught single-celled organisms many new protein words: these proteins are called "opsins," and they signal the presence of light. Opsins offer no visual sensation on their own, but are useful for pacing circadian rhythms and optimizing photosynthesis.

Next, many creatures formed a pigmented spot dense with opsins. The sensations created by these pigmented spots reveal how bright the world can be and convey the warning of a sudden shadow, but offer little other insight. Flatworms, starfish, and even some single-celled creatures, like euglena, have simple eyes like these today.

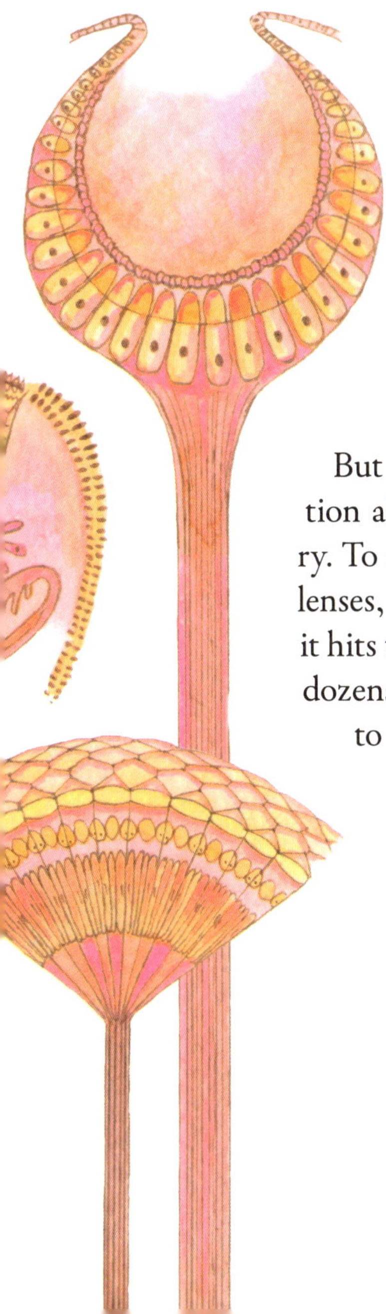

To reveal more about the location of objects, this spot had to be pinched into a shallow cup of receptors. With a cup, light that shines from different angles illuminates different parts of the spot inside the cup. As a nearby object reflects light, this eye-cup can capture clues about the object's location. The nautilus, a shelled relative of the octopus, has eyes like these.

But for such eyes, even though they can detect more information about where things are, the world still remains quite blurry. To focus Sun's reflection from every object, eyes next evolved lenses, clear proteins that bend light into a coherent image before it hits the pigmented, light-receiving cells. These lenses formed in dozens of ways, from the hard, external lens on the eyes of insects, to the spherical lens found in the box jellyfish, to the flattened, flexible lens in the human eye. We now know that different types of eyes have evolved as many as 65 separate times, sometimes starting over nearly from scratch. The one thing they have in common is their teacher: Sun.

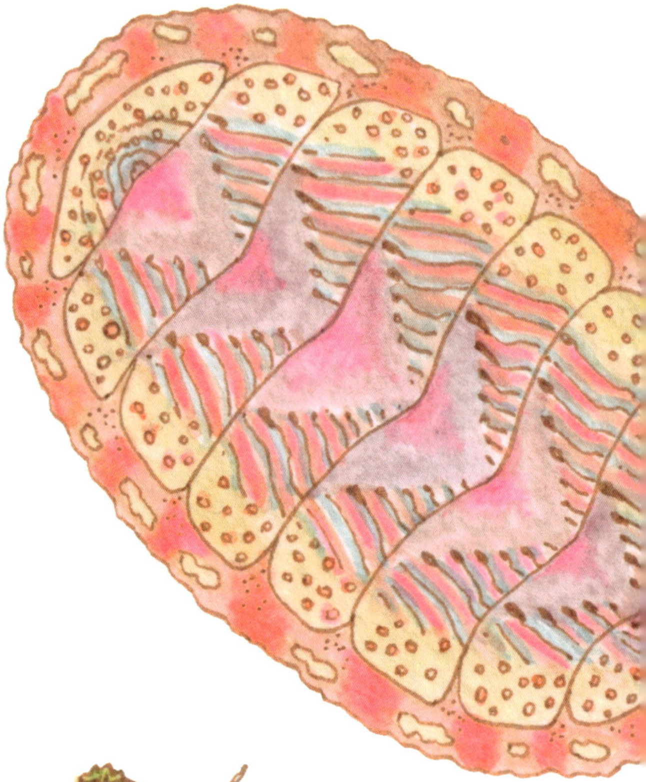

How many eyes do creatures need? Sometimes the answer is as many as they like. Creatures see through single eyes, pairs of eyes, and all kinds of other combinations, up to the unassuming chiton, a mollusk who sees the world through as many as a thousand ceramic eyes speckling the plates of its armored shell.

But depending on how one counts, insects could be said to have more. The compound eye of a dragonfly has up to 30,000 miniature eyes combined, each with its own lens and pigmented cells for detecting light.

There are even plankton known as "warnowiids" that use a tiny lens to focus light within their single-celled selves. If this lens allows them to "see," as scientists think it might, the warnowiid is a tiny eye with a life of its own.

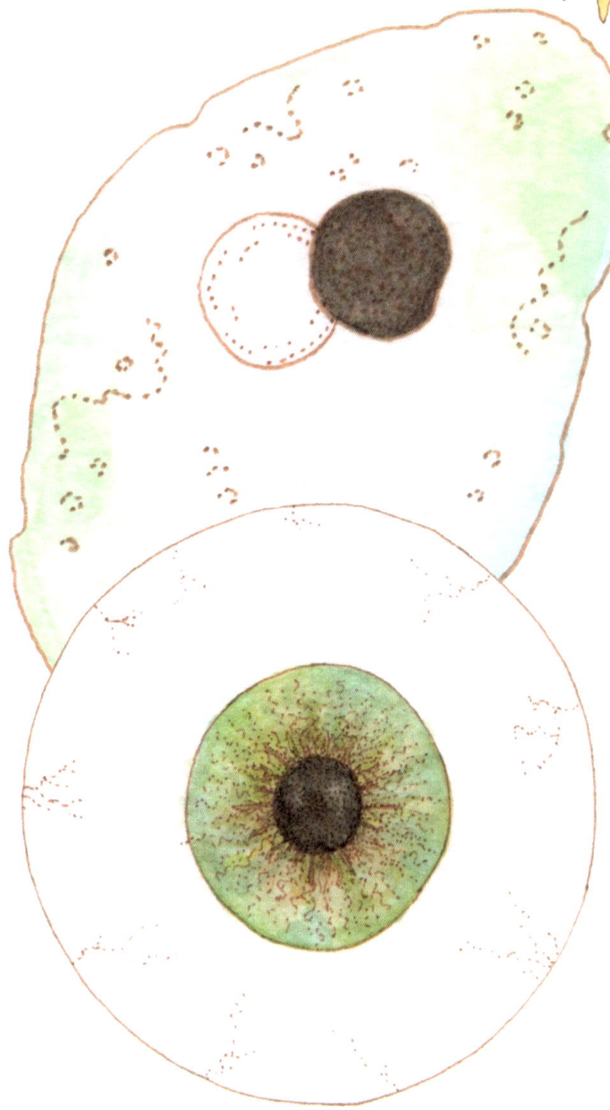

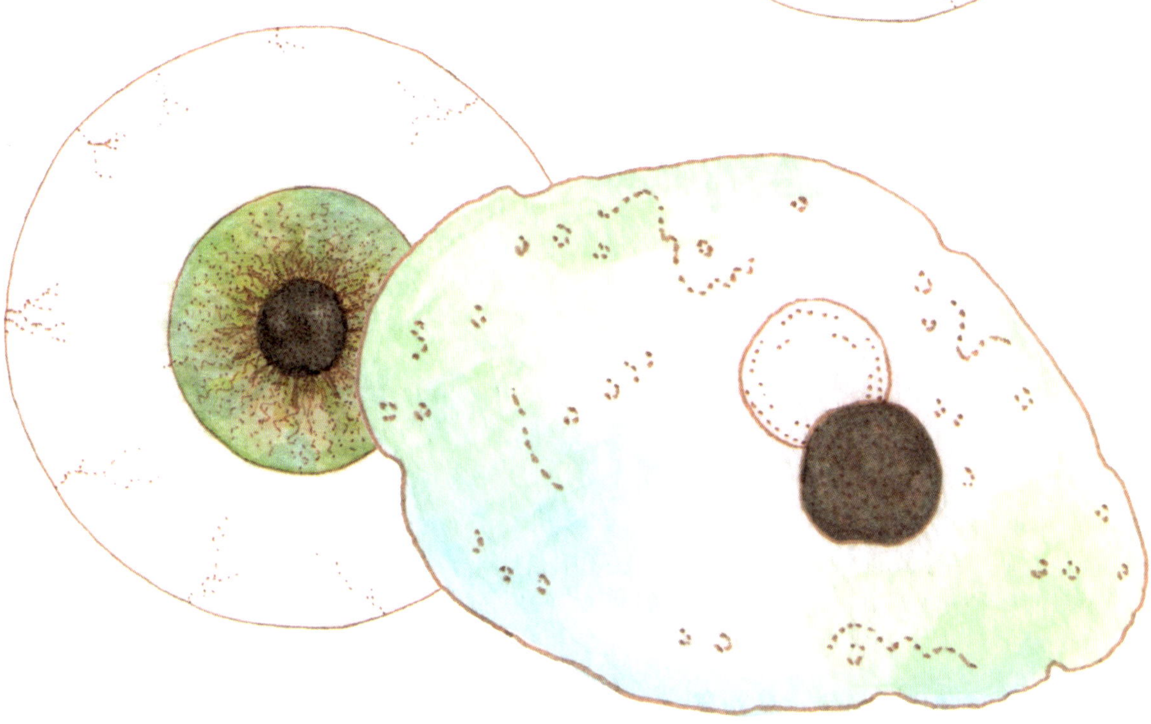

Evolutionarily, seeing light has been so important that one of our early vertebrate ancestors used more than two eyes to watch the world. Yes, the early precursor to mammals, a branch of life called "therapsids," actually had three eyes. But rather than making pictures of the world like the two eyes we possess, this third eye gazed sunward from the top of the head. What did this third eye see?

Ask the lizards and frogs, many of whom still today have what's called a "parietal eye" placed squarely on the tops of their heads. From there, the eye watches the changing light overhead. This helps lizards keep track of Sun's location across seasons and to sunbathe for the right amount of time each day.

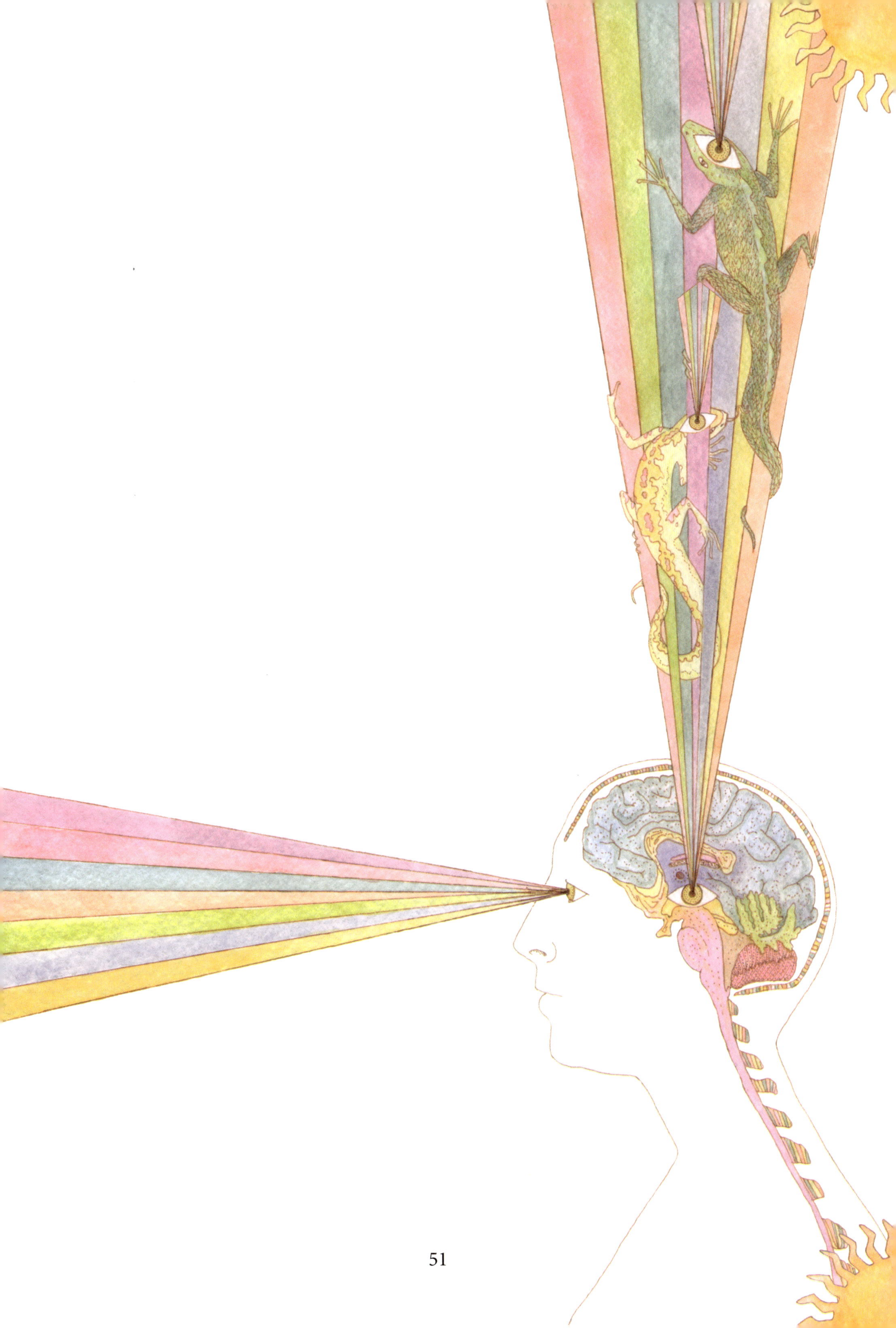

The third eye connects down to a mysterious part of the brain called the "pineal gland," which we still have today. The pineal gland is surprisingly symmetric and located in the exact center of the human brain. These facts captured the imagination of philosophers for centuries. Might this gland, as once suggested by René Descartes, contain the human soul and form the basis of human thought? Scientists now suspect that this unusual anatomy tells a different story: it is the remnant anatomy of that third eye. Incredibly, our pineal gland still makes opsin, the protein that detects light, even though it sits in darkness. Instead of watching the sky, the pineal gland now looks inward. It still plays a role relating to circadian rhythms, however, by producing melatonin to help us feel sleepy. But the signals it gets about light are no longer directly from the sky, but through our two eyes.

Through Sun's teachings, eyes evolved, and our own eyes have become so sensitive that we can see thousands of faint stars when we look up at the night sky. When stars are active and shining, there are reactions inside of them that turn hydrogen and helium into other types of atoms, like oxygen, nitrogen, and carbon. Then, when these stars die, they explode into space and cool into a cloud of dust, from which new stars and planets form. This process happened many times before the emergence of our own Solar System, but one cloud of stardust eventually formed our Sun and Earth, rich with the building blocks of life. This is why it's often said that our bodies are made from stardust.

But even after a star explodes to dust, its light continues to travel outward into space, just like water sprayed from a garden hose continues to fly through Air after the nozzle is shut off. This means that even after all this time, the light from the stars that made us is still traveling through the universe. By now, that light has likely reached a solar system billions of light-years away, where a different sun, for all we know, might have taught creatures to see.

Is someone, just now, watching the light from the stars we once were? And might they, like us, possess an inner sense for the grandeur of the universe?

PLANTS

We all understand the desire to taste a sweet food, to look at a dazzling color, or to smell a fresh aroma. Fascinatingly, Plants seem to understand something about these desires, too. Through the chemistry of photosynthesis, Plants support our food chain and make our oxygen, but the chemistry of their secondary metabolites—the catalog of thousands of complex chemicals that can entice or discourage animal interaction—form an especially unique and powerful teaching. These are the chemicals that make up fragrances, flavors, and pigments, as well as medicines. Many of these chemicals have pulled land-based creatures toward evolving new dimensions of smell, taste, touch, and sight. Indeed, over millions of years of chemical experimentation, Plants have taught us to expand our immediate sensory experience of the world.

Plants take root in soil, where they find necessary moisture and essential nutrients, like nitrogen. But the fact that they are stationary creates a number of challenges. The first is that of finding other Plants of the same species, which may not always be nearby, in order to exchange pollen and reproduce. Even if a plant resorts to self-pollination or cloning, staying in the same spot means that its offspring will soon compete with their parents for the same soil and sunlight. Being stationary also means that Plants can't run away from their predators. Therefore, Plants must create strong defenses against insects and herbivores who want to eat their stems, leaves, bark, and wood.

Consequently, Plants have evolved the ability to make thousands of unique chemicals that either attract or repel nearby animals. To reproduce, many Plants become sweet

and beautiful, growing pigmented flowers with chemical aromas to attract pollinators. They produce flavorful, bright fruits so the animals who eat these fruits can carry the seeds in their guts before dropping them down somewhere new. To defend against insects and herbivores, many Plants have also developed bad tastes, poisons, and compounds somewhere in between. The chemical "hexenol," for example, attracts wasps, which kill pests munching on a plant's leaves. Aromas, flavors, pigments, and poisons are what Plants do instead of moving around: Plants are mad chemists on a vine, inventing compounds of nearly every imaginable sort through endless trial and error. Collectively, these chemicals tell a vast array of stories about animal behavior, all captured in plant DNA. At the same time, the DNA of animals contains many stories about Plants.

What is it that's so alluring about a red rose? Our attraction to red roses might stem from our ancient primate makeup as fruit-eating mammals: we respond to red roses as if reliving an ancient memory. In this memory, a red fruit peeks through dense leaves, emanating a sweet perfume. Our primate ancestors needed to find fruiting Plants to survive. It has even been widely hypothesized that by putting pigments reflective of red light into their fruits, Plants taught early primates to see the color red. Plants had already developed red pigments to attract birds to their fruit, as birds had retained the ancient ability to see red that first developed in fish. This ability, however, was lost in mammals during a period when they were forced to live nocturnally. As a result, most other furry creatures (like cats and dogs) look at red and see only a grayish-brown. To better detect red fruits in a sea of green leaves, it is thought that each lineage of primate—prosimians, Old World primates, and New World primates—evolved different mutations in the proteins of the eye that sense color, enabling them to see red light in addition to blue and green. The smell of flowers also guided our ancestors to fruiting trees, likely teaching their olfactory systems to interpret these scents as enjoyable and sweet. It is these ancient sensory lessons of Plants that allow us to appreciate the scent of a fragrant red rose today.

Like all good teachers, Plants enter into dialogue with animals so that they can learn together. While it's in the interest of Plants to have their fruits eaten and pollen dispersed, they must also be able to protect themselves. Plants have evolved thousands of chemicals to warn animals against unwanted tastes. For example, the red chili pepper looks like any other ripened fruit, but the painful burning sensation caused by the chemical capsaicin contains a different message for mammals: "No chewing please—this fruit is not for you." Birds are a different story. While both birds and mammals have the protein that creates the sensation of burning, the gene is spelled slightly differently in birds, making them immune to the pepper's capsaicin. Birds will happily eat spicy peppers, and because birds do not chew, the seeds pass through their digestion system unharmed, to be spread far and wide. Despite the burning sensation, people in what is now Bolivia noticed 6,000 years ago that these peppers also prevented food from getting moldy, and so they began using them for food preservation. This discovery of a new use for the chili pepper's chemistry offered it an avenue to disperse and thrive: through human use and agriculture. Clearly, Plants can't predict the exact consequences of their chemical interventions; the chemicals might end up teaching a very different lesson from the one initially devised.

Moreover, the ancient people of Bolivia, like many people today, might also have enjoyed the surprising burn of the chili pepper. It offered a new sensation: a fire divorced from flame. Whenever the complex biochemistry of Plants interacts with a new species, the possible range of sensation expands. Many sensations will be unpleasant, but some will encourage interaction. Plants like tea and lavender are prized around the world for how they affect both mind and mood. Tea lends feelings of eagerness and creativity, while lavender brings a soothing sense of calm. But it's important to enjoy everything in moderation, as too much tea can produce unpleasant feelings of anxiety and a racing heart, while too much lavender can become toxic. In each case, the active ingredient (caffeine and linalool, respectively) acts as an insecticide for the plant, but because each of them appealed to us as a species, we have continued to use and enjoy them for thousands of years.

Other Plants offer dreamlike and transportive experiences. Plants like peyote and ayahuasca, for example, can bring feelings of awe and rapture that connect us to the wider world through an ecstatic sense of oneness. But hallucinogenic Plants can also produce nightmares, unwanted visions, bodily pain, and a terrifying loss of control. Consequently, from early religious festivals and indigenous rites up to the therapeutic and spiritual use of hallucinogens today, both great caution and great preparation are advised.

We often call such Plants "mind-altering," due to their ability to change people's perspectives. Today, these plants are also understood to increase the brain's natural mechanisms for making and removing neural connections, a process called "neural plasticity." But as mind-altering as hallucinogenic Plants may be, the fruiting trees that taught our primate ancestors to see red offered a more powerful mind-altering substance. For it was that red pigment that nurtured a new sensation—an almost psychedelic experience of new color—that continues to this day.

If DNA is an ancient text,
Plants are its poets.

They twist and turn with chemical creativity:
an intelligence by essence, a power by stem, leaf, and flower.

Yet, Plants somehow do all of this without exactly "knowing" what they are doing. Plants do not have nervous systems or brains, but what they do have are the stories written in their DNA—an accumulation of trial-and-error notes on how different chemicals helped or hurt their interactions with the animal world. Ultimately, these small chemical notes add up to a sweeping story about how animals behave, which involves moving around, being attracted to sweet substances, and a tendency to bite almost anything at least once.

Without eyes, Plants have taught us to see new colors.

Without tongues, they have taught us different flavors.

Without skin, they still seem to know our sensations of itchiness, coolness, pain, and heat.

Without noses, they have taught us the pleasant smells of rose, pine, and mint.

And without minds, they still know what serves to make us keen or calm.

Like bees humming around a flower, we too have hummed around Plants across the millennia, receptive to their next sensory lesson.

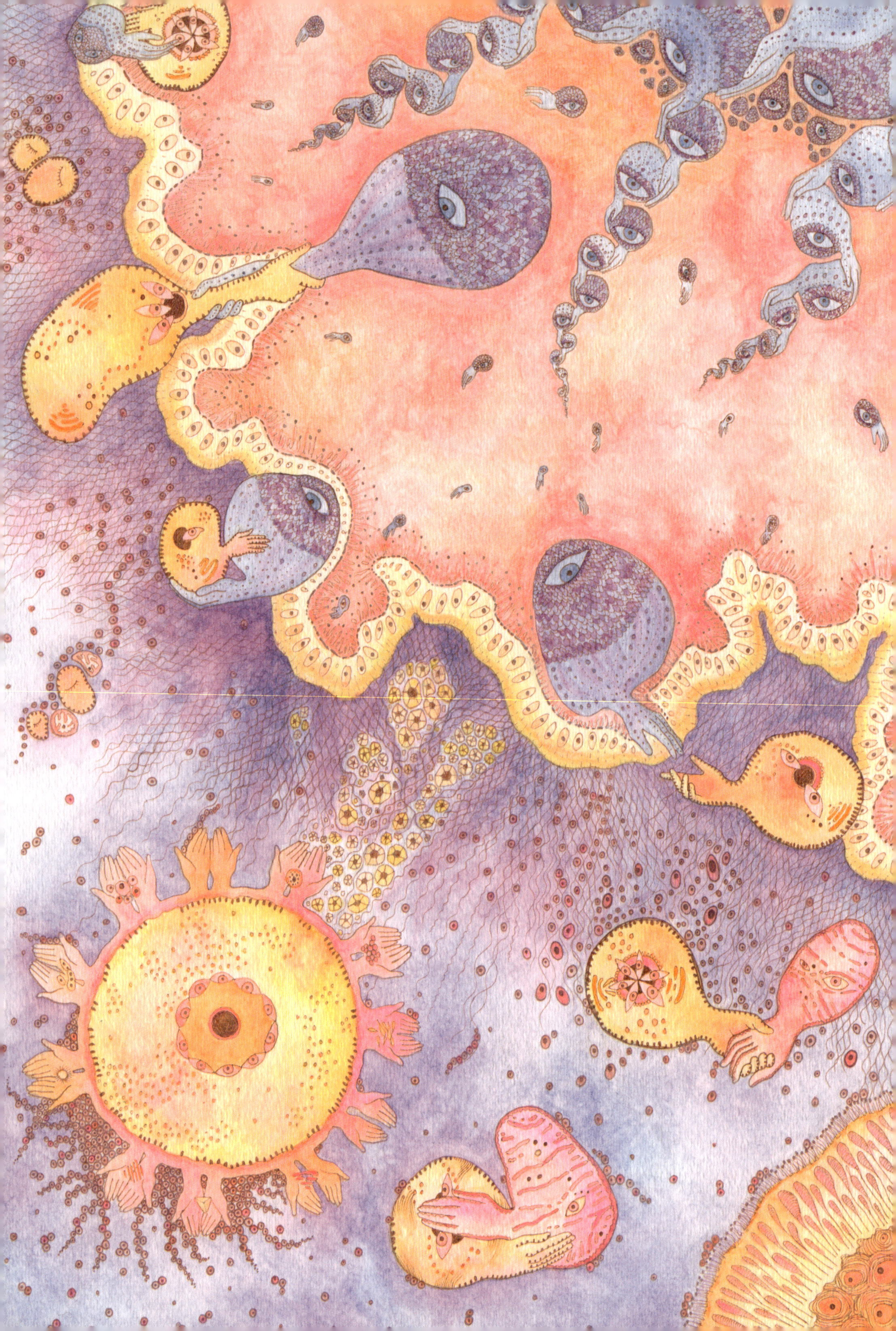

SYMBIONTS

There are some lessons that emerge only after creatures have had an opportunity to interact with one another over a very long period of time. Then, what began as two separate stories weaves together into a single story of interdependence. "Symbionts" are what we call members of different species who form tightly intertwined relationships over the course of their evolution. For example, the Star of Bethlehem orchid in Madagascar depends entirely on the Morgan's sphinx moth for pollination: this specific moth is the only known creature that can reach the nectar that lies deep inside the flower, possessing a tongue (or "proboscis") that is 11 inches long. This may seem like a fragile relationship, but nearly all life on Earth is sustained by one or more symbiotic relationships, making such interdependence fundamental to life itself. Indeed, it is because of these symbiotic relationships that humans carry more than their own story in their DNA; they also carry a story of mutual dependence—of symbiosis.

A very long time ago, when our most ancient ancestor was a single cell struggling to survive, that ancestor needed a boost of energy. Fortunately, another single-celled creature, a bacterium closely related to today's alphaproteobacteria, had more energy than it needed, having discovered how to harness oxygen and make energy. This bacterium was a bit like Prometheus, carrying a metabolic fire like the one discussed in the Air chapter. In return for this energy, our ancient ancestor shared nutrients. The two cells fused over time until, eventually, one lived inside the other.

This is the story of mitochondria, common components of our cells that are believed to come from a bacterial symbiont. Unlike our linear DNA, mitochondria still have their very own loop-shaped DNA, just like the DNA inside bacteria. The story of this collaborative relationship is then passed from mother to child, with mitochondrial DNA packaged inside an egg's fluids; a biological story of interdependence that stretches back more than one billion years, entirely unbroken.

Another ancient interdependence started when, after inviting mitochondria inside, one cell brought in a second neighbor—an odd, green bacterium that generated power from sunlight and is now called a "chloroplast." Together, these cells formed algae, the ancestor of all green Plants we see today. Chloroplasts are still inside each plant cell, harnessing the light of Sun and the carbon dioxide in Air to give Plants their green color. That means each plant cell is also home to two Symbionts: mitochondria and chloroplasts. A single plant cell contains the genetic story of all three.

But why stop there? As a type of plant, trees already contain these three stories, but nearly every tree also relies on a fungus. Trees invite fungi into their roots to help absorb nutrients like nitrogen and to form connections underground to other trees. Trees go on to provide habitats for hundreds of other creatures. Pretty soon, the network of a tree's symbiotic relationships looks a bit like a whole forest.

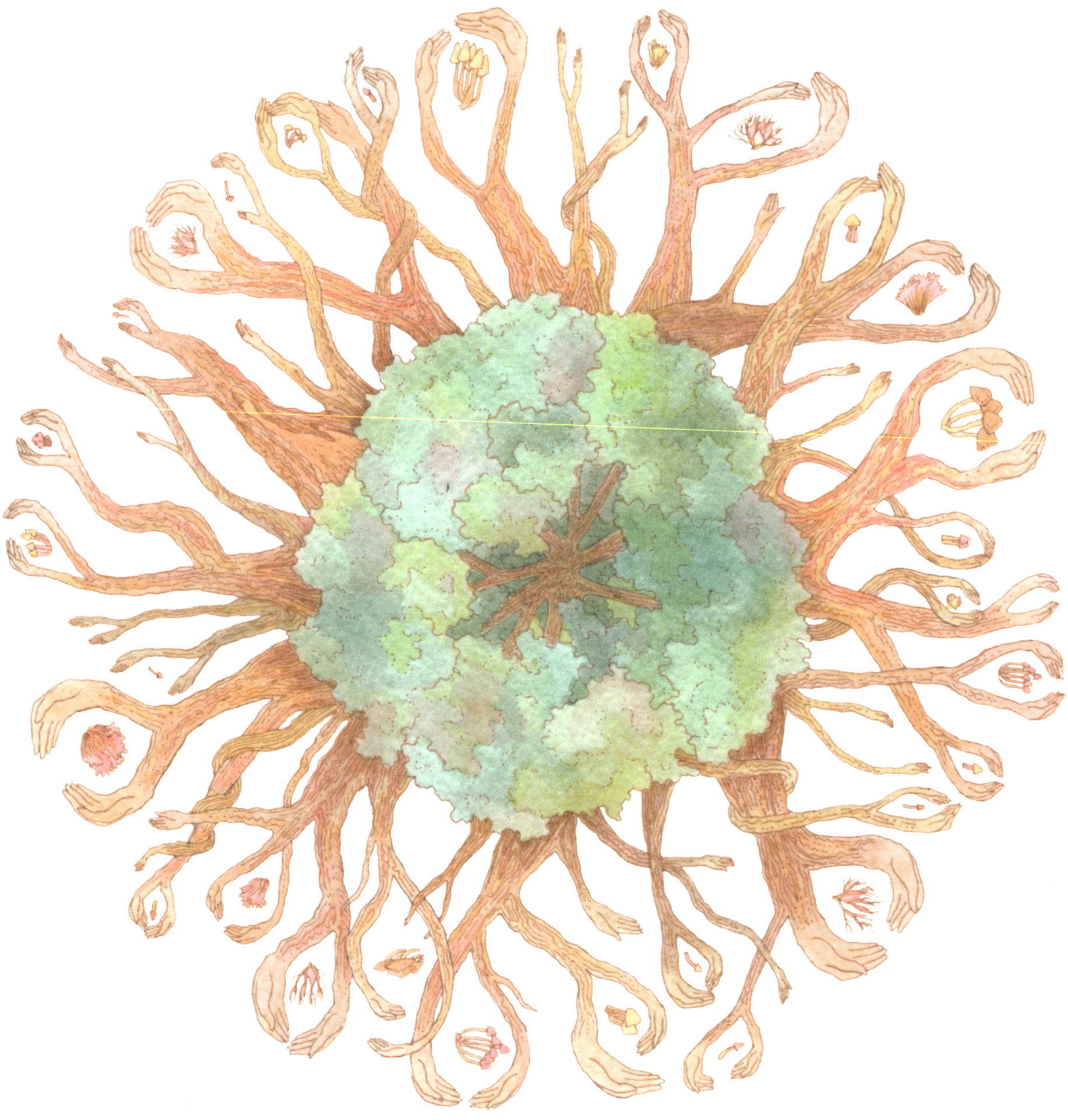

In the animal world, corals fill a similar role by supporting communities in bright, tropical oceans. One surprising thing about corals is that even though they are a type of animal called a "polyp," they perform photosynthesis. They do this by inviting algae called "zooxanthellae" inside their tentacles. The coral provides nutrients, protection, and carbon dioxide, while the algae makes food and oxygen from photosynthesis. The stony structures of coral provide habitats for hundreds of other sea creatures, making unique, thriving communities, similar to how trees make a forest. Without symbiosis, forests and coral reefs would not exist.

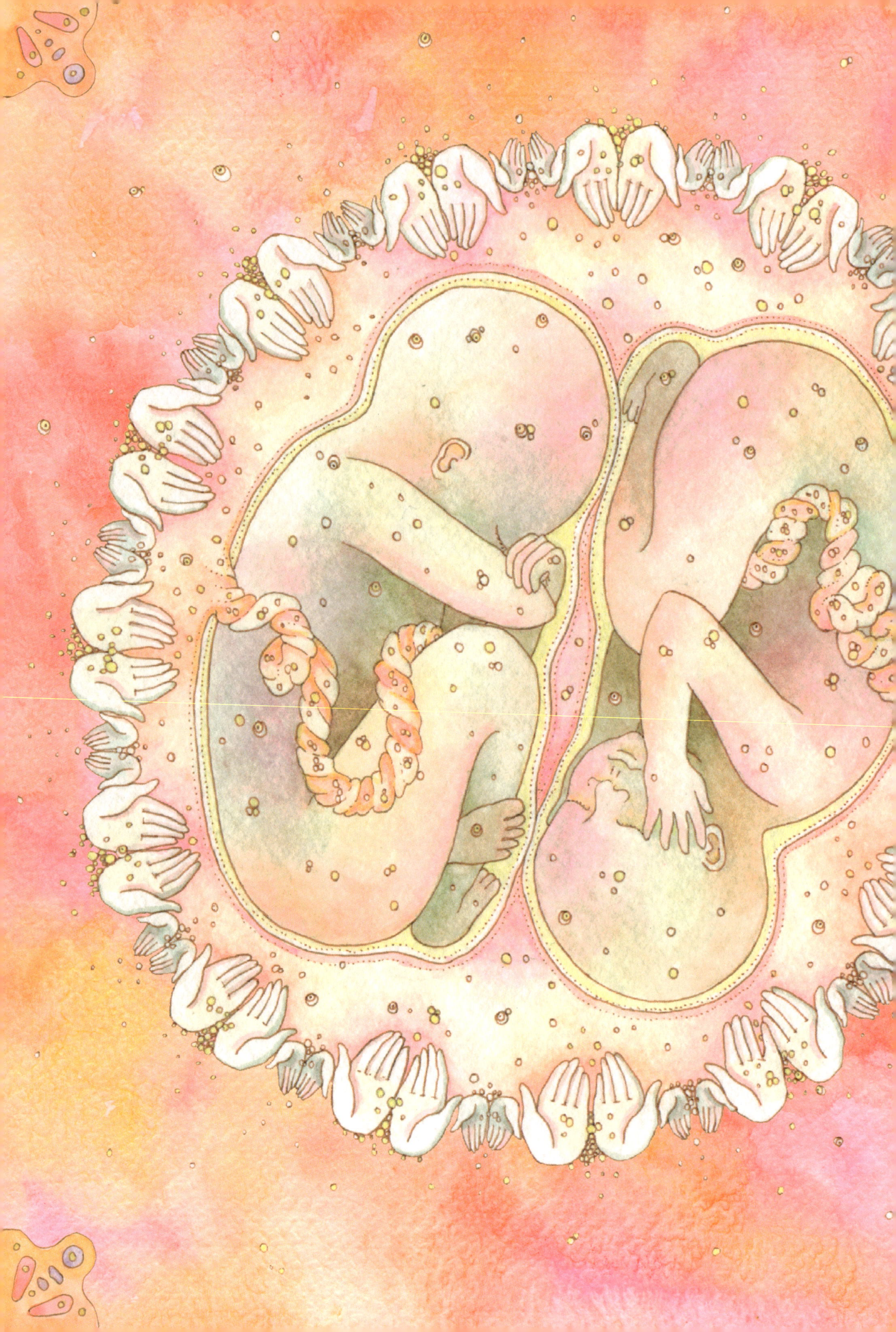

The human body has also derived many lessons from symbiosis. "Our" bodily cells are actually equally made up of Symbionts, with many measurements suggesting at least 50 percent of cells in the human body are bacteria and fungi. These trillions of microscopic organisms, called "bioflora," receive nutrients and a place to live. In return, they help clean our bodies, fight off harmful bacteria, and digest our food. Our bodies may even include cells from our mother—or twin, if we have one—in a common phenomenon called "chimerism." During pregnancy, the cells of mothers and babies often mix: a mother keeps a few cells from each baby, and a baby keeps some of their mother's cells. In the mother, a baby's stem cells can help repair injuries, while in a baby, the mother's cells help train the immune system. Twin siblings may swap a few cells as well. These close relatives continue carrying each other's cells for a long time, maybe even their whole lives.

Lessons from Symbionts continue outside of our bodies in the form of some of our most familiar companions. In fact, much of what we call "domestication"—the slow process of selecting Plants and animals we as a species found helpful, usually for agriculture—could also be understood as an evolutionary teaching of Symbionts. Dogs are descendants of wolves, and through the process of domestication, they have learned to help herd, protect, and hunt other animals alongside humans. Animals like cows are the descendants of the now-extinct species aurochs. Through the process of domestication, they came to provide us with milk and meat. These relationships have also changed us. The companionship of dairy animals caused some humans to evolve a tolerance for lactose, a sugar unique to milk. This allowed ancient humans to consume cow's milk into adulthood. Plants like broccoli, kale, Brussels sprouts, and cabbage are all descendants of wild cabbage, domesticated through years of agricultural practice. Even invertebrates like honeybees have traveled with us far and wide. Like a hermit crab decorating its shell with living sea anemones, ancient humans carried a community of familiar creatures on their journeys. In consequence, these communities were more likely to survive.

Symbionts provide a glimpse into the ancient truth that has sustained biology across the natural world: interdependence is the norm, not the exception. Even as species branch away on the Tree of Life, Symbionts weave these branches back together. Given enough time, the chloroplast fuses with algae, and the algae fuses with coral. Here, the teaching of Symbionts suggests that lasting survival emerges from the communities we make and the ecosystems to which we belong.

Is it a symbiotic relationship to breathe the oxygen in Air, put there by Plants, as they take in our old breath and make it new? Is it a symbiotic relationship to live sustainably with Ocean, watching Theia's tides come and go under the light of Sun? Our thriving world emerges from a dense thicket of Symbionts, which also offers a warning to us: when systems of symbiotic relationships are harmed, we too are harmed. If we destroy the world around us, we destroy parts of ourselves. It is only by sustaining all of life that we can expect to be sustained.

CONCLUSION

We are living in a time of profound ecological change. The planet is warming and Earth's creatures are currently going extinct at the fastest rate in 10 million years. This is happening in large part because humans are consuming land and natural resources too quickly, often destroying irreplaceable habitats in the process. For example, 70 percent of the deforestation in the Amazon rainforest has been linked to cattle farming, primarily for beef. At the current rate, as little as 20 percent of the rainforest will remain by the end of the 21st century. Inside that rainforest, there are thousands of creatures—insects, river dolphins, giant otters, jaguars, birds, fungi, plants—that live nowhere else in the world. Like all other life on earth, each of these creatures is exceptionally valuable. Not only do they work together in complex ways to sustain the rainforest and the indigenous people who live there, but they also carry unique stories captured in their DNA. It is only by sustaining this rich diversity that the story of life on our planet can be carried into the future.

As it stands, the lessons of the teachers gathered together in this book have been nearly forgotten. When human cultures move away from stories filled with wonder for the natural world, we lose our single greatest tool for preserving Earth's ecosystems. If we no longer tell stories about the forces that led to life on Earth, if we no longer stand in awe at the shared, mysterious gift of being alive, then the importance of these teachers is truly forgotten. Instead, let us remember what these ancient teachers have to impart to us, so we can fully reawaken to the natural world. Ours is a world filled with a beautiful, complex, and ancient aliveness—a living world that surrounds us and to which we all belong.

At this critical moment, when we can still change course, we must listen closely and get creative. We must imagine new ways to bring these forgotten teachers back into our human stories, so that they can illuminate the webs of interconnection that make us whole. Plants can only share their fruits, medicines, and insights while they are with us, and even then, only if we are receptive to them. Ocean can only nurture delicate experiments in life, like coral, when it is clean and cool. Air can only be replenished with oxygen by lush, thriving forests and an ocean filled with algae. These forgotten teachers serve to remind us that however rapidly we've changed our cultures and lifestyles through technology, we will always belong to a bigger, older story carried in the collective DNA of life on Earth. That story is profound and fragile. Modern biology, with technologies like DNA sequencing, can help us to appreciate our story more deeply, but to truly respect the forgotten teachers, we must change what we value in our daily lives. Economies and human-centric stories must shift. If we can't regain a deep respect and appreciation for Earth, the place to which we belong and that connects us all, we will deprive all who come next of beauty, mystery, wholeness, and, eventually, of life itself. It is time for us to attend to the world and all it has to tell us.

We are storytellers among storytellers,
trained by Forgotten Teachers.

The stories we tell from here
can evolve and return
us to what's important.

So let's begin telling stories
that Ocean can splash its fish toward,
like a beach of grunion under a full Moon.

Stories that Air itself might
breathe,
cool and forever,

Stories that glide and jump
with rhythms
like Theia's seasons and tides.

Stories that see a future
of looking backward
as easily as forward,
like the eyes of a dragonfly
under a bright Sun.

Stories that smell, taste, and burst
like flowering Plants,

and to which we can all connect,
like Symbionts.

If stories, like the story in DNA,
can last for four billion years,
what story will you choose to tell?

ARTIST'S NOTE

The Forgotten Teachers is an expression of my love for our living Earth. It is also an act of resistance against several powerful beliefs that shape the modern worldview.

The most devastating of these is the objectification and commodification of the more-than-human world. We reinforce these ideas in our language daily—even the most avid nature lovers and beloved children's books use the term "it" when referring to a living being. We've been conditioned to forget our position within a web of subjects. *The Forgotten Teachers* tells a different, much older story—one that celebrates the way in which humans are birthed from, shaped for, and ultimately taught by the dynamic systems that sustain life on Earth. Throughout the book, I use eyes to symbolize the ubiquity of awareness and hands to represent the universe's capacity to manifest life.

The Forgotten Teachers also challenges the belief that science and spirituality are mutually exclusive. Scientific knowledge can and should amplify, rather than diminish, our reverence for the great mysteries of existence. To this end, my illustrations draw inspiration from both analytic research and personal visions, dreams, and meditations. In art and design, the book echoes the style of medieval illuminated manuscripts, presenting scientific insights within a framework traditionally associated with spiritual works.

Finally, unlike most illustrated books, the text of *The Forgotten Teachers* was not written first. Text and image were created in dialogue, treated as equal partners in meaning-making. This collaborative process allowed us to blur the boundaries of art and science, making the poetic instructive and the factual enchanting. According to a quotation often attributed to Albert Einstein, there are only two ways to live your life: "One is as though nothing is a miracle. The other is as though everything is a miracle." It is my hope that *The Forgotten Teachers* makes the latter irresistible.

BIBLIOGRAPHY

Asner, Gregory P., Scott R. Loarie, and Ursula Heyder. 2010. "Combined Effects of Climate and Land-Use Change on the Future of Humid Tropical Forests." *Conservation Letters* 3 (6): 395–403. https://doi.org/10.1111/j.1755-263X.2010.00133.x.\

Beall, M. H., J. P. H. M. van den Wijngaard, M. J. C. van Gemert, and M. G. Ross. 2007. "Amniotic Fluid Water Dynamics." *Placenta* 28 (8): 816–23. https://doi.org/10.1016/j.placenta.2006.11.009.

Benoit, Julien, Fernando Abdala, Paul R. Manger, and Bruce S. Rubidge. 2016. "The Sixth Sense in Mammalian Forerunners: Variability of the Parietal Foramen and the Evolution of the Pineal Eye in South African Permo-Triassic Eutheriodont Therapsids." *Acta Palaeontologica Polonica* 61 (4): 777–89. https://doi.org/10.4202/app.00219.2015.

Canup, Robin M., and Erik Asphaug. 2001. "Origin of the Moon in a Giant Impact near the End of the Earth's Formation." *Nature* 412 (6848): 708–12. https://doi.org/10.1038/35089010.

Carvalho, Livia S., Daniel M. A. Pessoa, Jessica K. Mountford, Wayne I. L. Davies, and David M. Hunt. 2017. "The Genetic and Evolutionary Drives behind Primate Color Vision." *Frontiers in Ecology and Evolution* 5 (April). https://doi.org/10.3389/fevo.2017.00034.

"Cellular Respiration." 2024. In Wikipedia. https://en.wikipedia.org/w/index.php?title=Cellular_respiration&oldid=1230158300.

Chrétien, Dominique, Paule Bénit, Hyung-Ho Ha, Susanne Keipert, Riyad El-Khoury, Young-Tae Chang, Martin Jastroch, Howard T. Jacobs, Pierre Rustin, and Malgorzata Rak. 2018. "Mitochondria Are Physiologically Maintained at Close to 50 °C." *PLOS Biology* 16 (1): e2003992. https://doi.org/10.1371/journal.pbio.2003992.

Chu, Ying, Bruce E. Cohen, and Huai-hu Chuang. 2020. "A Single TRPV1 Amino Acid Controls Species Sensitivity to Capsaicin." *Scientific Reports* 10 (1): 8038. https://doi.org/10.1038/s41598-020-64584-2.

Davis, Tamara M., and Charles H. Lineweaver. 2004. "Expanding Confusion: Common Misconceptions of Cosmological Horizons and the Superluminal Expansion of the Universe." *Publications of the Astronomical Society of Australia* 21 (1): 97–109. https://doi.org/10.1071/AS03040.

Dawe, Gavin S, Xiao Wei Tan, and Zhi-Cheng Xiao. 2007. "Cell Migration from Baby to Mother." *Cell Adhesion & Migration* 1 (1): 19–27.

De La Peña, Marcos, and Inmaculada García-Robles. 2010. "Intronic Hammerhead Ribozymes Are Ultraconserved in the Human Genome." *EMBO Reports* 11 (9): 711–16. https://doi.org/10.1038/embor.2010.100.

Decker, Jared E., Stephanie D. McKay, Megan M. Rolf, JaeWoo Kim, Antonio Molina Alcalá, Tad S. Sonstegard, Olivier Hanotte, et al. 2014. "Worldwide Patterns of Ancestry, Divergence, and Admixture in Domesticated Cattle." *PLOS Genetics* 10 (3): e1004254. https://doi.org/10.1371/journal.pgen.1004254.

Descartes, René. 1955. *The Passions of the Soul.* Newcomb Livraria Press.

England, Jeremy L. 2013. "Statistical Physics of Self-Replication." *The Journal of Chemical Physics* 139 (12): 121923. https://doi.org/10.1063/1.4818538.

Evans, Martin. 2022. "Geomorphology and the Fast Carbon Cycle." In *Geomorphology and the Carbon Cycle*, 12–36. Hoboken, NJ, USA: John Wiley & Sons, Inc. https://doi.org/10.1002/9781119393290.ch2.

Falcone Ferreyra, Maria L., Sebastian P. Rius, and Paula Casati. 2012. "Flavonoids: Biosynthesis, Biological Functions, and Biotechnological Applications." *Frontiers in Plant Science* 3:222. https://doi.org/10.3389/fpls.2012.00222.

Fearnside, P. M. 2005. "Deforestation in Brazilian Amazonia: History, Rates, and Consequences." *Conservation Biology* 19 (3): 680–88. https://doi.org/10.1111/j.1523-1739.2005.00697.x.

Frisdal, Aude, and Paul A. Trainor. 2014. "Development and Evolution of the Pharyngeal Apparatus." *WIREs Developmental Biology* 3 (6): 403–18. https://doi.org/10.1002/wdev.147.

Gai, Zhikun, Min Zhu, Per E. Ahlberg, and Philip C. J. Donoghue. 2022. "The Evolution of the Spiracular Region From Jawless Fishes to Tetrapods." *Frontiers in Ecology and Evolution* 10 (May). https://doi.org/10.3389/fevo.2022.887172.

Greene, Brian. 2020. *Until the End of Time: Mind, Matter, and Our Search for Meaning in an Evolving Universe.* Knopf Doubleday Publishing Group.

Hammann, Christian, Andrej Luptak, Jonathan Perreault, and Marcos de la Peña. 2012. "The Ubiquitous Hammerhead Ribozyme." *RNA* 18 (5): 871–85. https://doi.org/10.1261/rna.031401.111.

Hayakawa, Shiho, Yasuharu Takaku, Jung Shan Hwang, Takeo Horiguchi, Hiroshi Suga, Walter Gehring, Kazuho Ikeo, and Takashi Gojobori. 2015. "Function and Evolutionary Origin of Unicellular Camera-Type Eye Structure." Edited by Simonetta Gribaldo. *PLOS One* 10 (3): e0118415. https://doi.org/10.1371/journal.pone.0118415.

Heesy, Christopher P., and Margaret I. Hall. 2010. "The Nocturnal Bottleneck and the Evolution of Mammalian Vision." *Brain Behavior and Evolution* 75 (3): 195–203. https://doi.org/10.1159/000314278.

Holland, Heinrich D. 2006. "The Oxygenation of the Atmosphere and Oceans." *Philosophical Transactions of the Royal Society B: Biological Sciences* 361 (1470): 903–15. https://doi.org/10.1098/rstb.2006.1838.

Huang, Guangping, Yubo Zhang, Wei Zhang, and Fuwen Wei. 2024. "Genetic Mechanisms of Animal Camouflage: An Interdisciplinary Perspective." *Trends in Genetics: TIG* 40 (7): 613–20. https://doi.org/10.1016/j.tig.2024.03.009.

Kasperski, Andrzej, and Renata Kasperska. 2021. "Study on Attractors during Organism Evolution." *Scientific Reports* 11 (1): 9637. https://doi.org/10.1038/s41598-021-89001-0.

Kinder, Jeremy M., Ina A. Stelzer, Petra C. Arck, and Sing Sing Way. 2017. "Immunological Implications of Pregnancy-Induced Microchimerism." *Nature Reviews Immunology* 17 (8): 483–94. https://doi.org/10.1038/nri.2017.38.

Krebs, John R. 2009. "The Gourmet Ape: Evolution and Human Food Preferences." *American Journal of Clinical Nutrition* 90 (3): 707S-711S. https://doi.org/10.3945/ajcn.2009.27462B.

Kumar, Vinod, ed. 2017. *Biological Timekeeping: Clocks, Rhythms and Behaviour.* New Delhi: Springer India. https://doi.org/10.1007/978-81-322-3688-7.

LaJeunesse, Todd C., John Everett Parkinson, Paul W. Gabrielson, Hae Jin Jeong, James Davis Reimer, Christian R. Voolstra, and Scott R. Santos. 2018. "Systematic Revision of Symbiodiniaceae Highlights the Antiquity and Diversity of Coral Endosymbionts." *Current Biology* 28 (16): 2570-+. https://doi.org/10.1016/j.cub.2018.07.008.

Lamb, Trevor D., Shaun P. Collin, and Edward N. Pugh. 2007. "Evolution of the Vertebrate Eye: Opsins, Photoreceptors, Retina and Eye Cup." *Nature Reviews Neuroscience* 8 (12): 960–76. https://doi.org/10.1038/nrn2283.

Land, M. F., and R. D. Fernald. 1992. "The Evolution of Eyes." *Annual Review of Neuroscience* 15:1–29. https://doi.org/10.1146/annurev.ne.15.030192.000245.

Lau, Sally C. Y., Nerida G. Wilson, Nicholas R. Golledge, Tim R. Naish, Phillip C. Watts, Catarina N. S. Silva, Ira R. Cooke, et al. 2023. "Genomic Evidence for West Antarctic Ice Sheet Collapse during the Last Interglacial." *Science* 382 (6677): 1384–89. https://doi.org/10.1126/science.ade0664.

Li, Ling, Matthew J. Connors, Mathias Kolle, Grant T. England, Daniel I. Speiser, Xianghui Xiao, Joanna Aizenberg, and Christine Ortiz. 2015. "Multifunctionality of Chiton Biomineralized Armor with an Integrated Visual System." *Science* 350 (6263): 952–56. https://doi.org/10.1126/science.aad1246.

Li, Wei, Lei Ma, Guang Yang, and Wen-Biao Gan. 2017. "REM Sleep Selectively Prunes and Maintains New Synapses in Development and Learning." *Nature Neuroscience* 20 (3): 427–37. https://doi.org/10.1038/nn.4479.

Lukasiewicz, Kacper, Jacob J. Baker, Yi Zuo, and Ju Lu. 2021. "Serotonergic Psychedelics in Neural Plasticity." *Frontiers in Molecular Neuroscience* 14 (October). https://doi.org/10.3389/fnmol.2021.748359.

Martin, Karen, Karen Bailey, Cassadie Moravek, and Kjirsten Carlson. 2011. "Taking the Plunge: California Grunion Embryos Emerge Rapidly with Environmentally Cued Hatching." *Integrative and Comparative Biology* 51 (1): 26–37. https://doi.org/10.1093/icb/icr037.

Martin, William, John Baross, Deborah Kelley, and Michael J. Russell. 2008. "Hydrothermal Vents and the Origin of Life." *Nature Reviews Microbiology* 6 (11): 805–14. https://doi.org/10.1038/nrmicro1991.

Mead, Jere. 1960. "Control of Respiratory Frequency." *Journal of Applied Physiology* 15 (3): 325–36. https://doi.org/10.1152/jappl.1960.15.3.325.

Meyer, Axel, Siegfried Schloissnig, Paolo Franchini, Kang Du, Joost M. Woltering, Iker Irisarri, Wai Yee Wong, et al. 2021. "Giant Lungfish Genome Elucidates the Conquest of Land by Vertebrates." *Nature* 590 (7845): 284–89. https://doi.org/10.1038/s41586-021-03198-8.

Mithoefer, Axel, and Wilhelm Boland. 2012. "Plant Defense Against Herbivores: Chemical Aspects." *Annual Review of Plant Biology*, edited by S. S. Merchant, 63:431–50. Palo Alto: Annual Reviews. https://doi.org/10.1146/annurev-arplant-042110-103854.

Morales-Garcia, Jose A., Mario de la Fuente Revenga, Sandra Alonso-Gil, Maria Isabel Rodriguez-Franco, Amanda Feilding, Ana Perez-Castillo, and Jordi Riba. 2017. "The Alkaloids of Banisteriopsis Caapi, the Plant Source of the Amazonian Hallucinogen Ayahuasca, Stimulate Adult Neurogenesis in Vitro." *Scientific Reports* 7 (July):5309. https://doi.org/10.1038/s41598-017-05407-9.

Mulkidjanian, Armen Y., Michael Y. Galperin, and Eugene V. Koonin. 2009. "Co-Evolution of Primordial Membranes and Membrane Proteins." *Trends in Biochemical Sciences* 34 (4): 206–15. https://doi.org/10.1016/j.tibs.2009.01.005.

Orgel, L. E. 2004. "Prebiotic Chemistry and the Origin of the RNA World." *Critical Reviews in Biochemistry and Molecular Biology* 39 (2): 99–123. https://doi.org/10.1080/10409230490460765.
Papineau, Dominic, Jeffrey J. Walker, Stephen J. Mojzsis, and Norman R. Pace. 2005.

"Composition and Structure of Microbial Communities from Stromatolites of Hamelin Pool in Shark Bay, Western Australia." *Applied and Environmental Microbiology* 71 (8): 4822–32. https://doi.org/10.1128/AEM.71.8.4822-4832.2005.

Parvizi, Elahe, Dave Craw, and Jonathan M. Waters. 2019. "Kelp DNA Records Late Holocene Paleoseismic Uplift of Coastline, Southeastern New Zealand." *Earth and Planetary Science Letters* 520 (August):18–25. https://doi.org/10.1016/j.epsl.2019.05.034.

Pillay, Rajeev, Michelle Venter, Jose Aragon-Osejo, Pamela González-del-Pliego, Andrew J Hansen, James EM Watson, and Oscar Venter. 2022. "Tropical Forests Are Home to over Half of the World's Vertebrate Species." *Frontiers in Ecology and the Environment* 20 (1): 10–15. https://doi.org/10.1002/fee.2420.

Puttonen, Eetu, Christian Briese, Gottfried Mandlburger, Martin Wieser, Martin Pfennigbauer, András Zlinszky, and Norbert Pfeifer. 2016. "Quantification of Overnight Movement of Birch (Betula Pendula) Branches and Foliage with Short Interval Terrestrial Laser Scanning." *Frontiers in Plant Science* 7 (February). https://doi.org/10.3389/fpls.2016.00222.

Robler, Daniela C., Kris Kim, Massimo De Agro, Alex Jordan, C. Giovanni Galizia, and Paul S. Shamble. 2022. "Regularly Occurring Bouts of Retinal Movements Suggest an REM Sleep-like State in Jumping Spiders." *Proceedings of the National Academy of Sciences of the United States of America* 119 (33): e2204754119. https://doi.org/10.1073/pnas.2204754119.

Rolfe, D. F., and G. C. Brown. 1997. "Cellular Energy Utilization and Molecular Origin of Standard Metabolic Rate in Mammals." *Physiological Reviews* 77 (3): 731–58. https://doi.org/10.1152/physrev.1997.77.3.731.

Rull, Valentí. 2022. "Biodiversity Crisis or Sixth Mass Extinction?" *EMBO Reports* 23 (1): e54193. https://doi.org/10.15252/embr.202154193.

Sachs, Joel L., Ryan G. Skophammer, and John U. Regus. 2011. "Evolutionary Transitions in Bacterial Symbiosis." *Proceedings of the National Academy of Sciences of the United States of America* 108 (Suppl 2): 10800–807. https://doi.org/10.1073/pnas.1100304108.

Satoh, Aya, and Yohey Terai. 2019. "Circatidal Gene Expression in the Mangrove Cricket Apteronemobius Asahinai." *Scientific Reports* 9 (1): 3719. https://doi.org/10.1038/s41598-019-40197-2.

Scaldaferro, Marisel A, Gloria E Barboza, and M Cristina Acosta. 2018. "Evolutionary History of the Chili Pepper Capsicum Baccatum L. (Solanaceae): Domestication in South America and Natural Diversification in the Seasonally Dry Tropical Forests." *Biological Journal of the Linnean Society* 124 (3): 466–78. https://doi.org/10.1093/biolinnean/bly062.

Scott, Andrew C., and Ian J. Glasspool. 2006. "The Diversification of Paleozoic Fire Systems and Fluctuations in Atmospheric Oxygen Concentration." Proceedings of the National Academy of Sciences of the United States of America 103 (29): 10861–65. https://doi.org/10.1073/pnas.0604090103.

Siegel, J. M., P. R. Manger, R. Nienhuis, H. M. Fahringer, and J. D. Pettigrew. 1998. "Monotremes and the Evolution of Rapid Eye Movement Sleep." *Philosophical Transactions of the Royal Society of London Series B-Biological Sciences* 353 (1372): 1147–57. https://doi.org/10.1098/rstb.1998.0272.

Stansell, Zachary, Katie Hyma, Jonathan Fresnedo-Ramírez, Qi Sun, Sharon Mitchell, Thomas Björkman, and Jian Hua. 2018. "Genotyping-by-Sequencing of Brassica Oleracea Vegetables Reveals Unique Phylogenetic Patterns, Population Structure and Domestication Footprints." *Horticulture Research* 5 (July):38. https://doi.org/10.1038/s41438-018-0040-3.

Stickgold, R., J. A. Hobson, R. Fosse, and M. Fosse. 2001. "Sleep, Learning, and Dreams: Off-Line Memory Reprocessing." *Science* 294 (5544): 1052–57. https://doi.org/10.1126/science.1063530.

Sussman, Robert W. 1991. "Primate Origins and the Evolution of Angiosperms." *American Journal of Primatology* 23 (4): 209–23. https://doi.org/10.1002/ajp.1350230402.

Tanaka, Yoshikazu, Nobuhiro Sasaki, and Akemi Ohmiya. 2008. "Biosynthesis of Plant Pigments: Anthocyanins, Betalains and Carotenoids." *Plant Journal* 54 (4): 733–49. https://doi.org/10.1111/j.1365-313X.2008.03447.x.

Thompson, Will F., and Julia Bell Thompson. 1919. "Fish Bulletin No. 3. The Spawning of the Grunion (Leuresthes Tenuis)," July. https://escholarship.org/uc/item/32f9j2gk.

Tosini, Gianluca. 1997. "The Pineal Complex of Reptiles: Physiological and Behavioral Roles." *Ethology Ecology & Evolution* 9 (4): 313–33. https://doi.org/10.1080/08927014.1997.9522875.

Vigh, B., M. J. Manzano, A. Zádori, C. L. Frank, A. Lukáts, P. Röhlich, A. Szél, and C. Dávid. 2002. "Nonvisual Photoreceptors of the Deep Brain, Pineal Organs and Retina." *Histology and Histopathology* 17 (2): 555–90. https://doi.org/10.14670/HH-17.555.

Wei, Jianing, Lizhong Wang, Junwei Zhu, Sufang Zhang, Owi I. Nandi, and Le Kang. 2007. "Plants Attract Parasitic Wasps to Defend Themselves against Insect Pests by Releasing Hexenol." *PLOS One* 2 (9): e852. https://doi.org/10.1371/journal.pone.0000852.

Weiss, Madeline C., Filipa L. Sousa, Natalia Mrnjavac, Sinje Neukirchen, Mayo Roettger, Shijulal Nelson-Sathi, and William F. Martin. 2016. "The Physiology and Habitat of the Last Universal Common Ancestor." *Nature Microbiology* 1 (9): 1–8. https://doi.org/10.1038/nmicrobiol.2016.116.

Welch, Brian, Dan Coe, Erik Zackrisson, S. E. de Mink, Swara Ravindranath, Jay Anderson, Gabriel Brammer, et al. 2022. "JWST Imaging of Earendel, the Extremely Magnified Star at Redshift z = 6.2." *The Astrophysical Journal Letters* 940 (1): L1. https://doi.org/10.3847/2041-8213/ac9d39.

Wooding, Stephen. 2005. "Evolution: A Study in Bad Taste?" *Current Biology* 15 (19): R805–7. https://doi.org/10.1016/j.cub.2005.09.021.

Yuan, Qian, Mingming Li, Steven J. Desch, Byeongkwan Ko, Hongping Deng, Edward J. Garnero, Travis S. J. Gabriel, et al. 2023. "Moon-Forming Impactor as a Source of Earth's Basal Mantle Anomalies." *Nature* 623 (7985): 95–99. https://doi.org/10.1038/s41586-023-06589-1.

Zürcher, Ernst, Maria-Giulia Cantiani, Francesco Sorbetti-Guerri, and Denis Michel. 1998. "Tree Stem Diameters Fluctuate with Tide." *Nature* 392 (6677): 665–66. https://doi.org/10.1038/33570.

ACKNOWLEDGMENTS

I would like to thank Claudia Biçen for the amazing discussions that went into writing and illustrating this book and for her commitment to clarifying and shaping these ideas. I would also like to thank Claudia Zoe Bedrick and Emilie Robert Wong at Enchanted Lion for their patience and insight in editing *The Forgotten Teachers*, as well as James Ingoldsby, Margaret Krauss, Ryan Woodring, and John Soat for feedback and suggestions. I am thankful for the support of my family and friends, especially my wife Melanie, who watched our children for countless hours each morning as I wrote. Last but not least, thank you to our generous Kickstarter backers, who pledged toward the printing costs of the book. Without all of your support, this book would not exist. —*Brian Isett*

Thank you to the living Earth for teaching me to pay attention, be humble, and love. This book is for you. Thank you also to Earth's humans. Brian, thank you for the countless conversations that sparked sacred visions in my mind. Bryce, thank you for always encouraging me to trust in myself and create strange things for no other reason than joy. My family, thank you for raising me within an ecosystem infused with curiosity, wonder, and love. Don Louie, thank you for keeping the magic alive. Claudia Zoe Bedrick, thank you for believing in this book and helping us share it with the world.
—*Claudia Biçen*